CELEBRATING THE FAMILY NAME OF HUANG

Celebrating the Family Name of Huang

Walter the Educator

Silent King Books
a WhichHead Entertainment Imprint

Copyright © 2024 by Walter the Educator

All rights reserved. No part of this book may be reproduced in any manner whatsoever without written permission except in the case of brief quotations embodied in critical articles and reviews.

First Printing, 2024

Disclaimer

This book is a literary work; the story is not about specific persons, locations, situations, and/or circumstances unless mentioned in a historical context. Any resemblance to real persons, locations, situations, and/or circumstances is coincidental. This book is for entertainment and informational purposes only. The author and publisher offer this information without warranties expressed or implied. No matter the grounds, neither the author nor the publisher will be accountable for any losses, injuries, or other damages caused by the reader's use of this book. The use of this book acknowledges an understanding and acceptance of this disclaimer.

Celebrating the Family Name of Huang is a memory book that belongs to the Celebrating Family Name Book Series by Walter the Educator. Collect them all and more books at WaltertheEducator.com

USE THE EXTRA SPACE TO DOCUMENT YOUR FAMILY MEMORIES THROUGHOUT THE YEARS

HUANG

In fields where sunlight meets the earth,

The name of Huang finds noble birth.

A golden thread through history's weave,

A name of honor, hearts believe.

Born of mountains, bold and grand,

The Huang name echoes across the land.

From rivers wide to forests deep,

Their legacy, a vow to keep.

Through ancient scrolls and songs of old,

The Huang name shines like purest gold.

A beacon bright, a steady flame,

Forever cherished, their timeless name.

From scholars wise with ink-stained hands,

To farmers tending fertile lands,

The Huang name bridges worlds apart,

With steady will and open heart.

Builders of futures, dreamers of light,

The Huang name rises through the night.

In every deed, in every care,

A legacy treasured everywhere.

Through changing tides, they held their ground,

In Huang's great name, resolve is found.

A family steadfast, strong, and true,

Their roots run deep, their vision new.

In art and craft, their mark is laid,

In every stone, in every blade.

The Huang name whispers through the air,

A symbol bold, beyond compare.

Through storms of life, through skies of blue,

The Huang name carries strength anew.

With wisdom drawn from earth and sky,

Their spirit soars, it cannot die.

Each generation lifts the flame,

To honor all who bore the name.

Their unity, a bond so tight,

A shining path, a guiding light.

So raise your voice, let praises ring,

For Huang, the name of which we sing.

A family bold, with hearts of gold,

Their story forever, proudly told.

ABOUT THE CREATOR

Walter the Educator is one of the pseudonyms for Walter Anderson. Formally educated in Chemistry, Business, and Education, he is an educator, an author, a diverse entrepreneur, and he is the son of a disabled war veteran. "Walter the Educator" shares his time between educating and creating. He holds interests and owns several creative projects that entertain, enlighten, enhance, and educate, hoping to inspire and motivate you. Follow, find new works, and stay up to date with Walter the Educator™

at WaltertheEducator.com

www.ingramcontent.com/pod-product-compliance
Lightning Source LLC
LaVergne TN
LVHW012051070526
838201LV00082B/3911